D0959965

Elizabeth Taylor

A Passion for Life

The Wit and Wisdom of a Legend

Joseph Papa

HARPER
DESIGN

An Imprint of HarperCollinsPublishers

Elizabeth Taylor: A Passion for Life

HarperCollins books may be purchased for educational, business, or sales promotional use. For information please write: Special Markets Department, HarperCollins*Publishers*, 10 East 53rd Street, New York, **NY** 10022.

First published in 2011 by
Harper Design
An Imprint of HarperCollins*Publishers*
10 East 53rd Street
New York, NY 10022
Tel: (212) 207-7000
Fax: (212) 207-7654
harperdesign@harpercollins.com

Distributed throughout the world by
HarperCollins*Publishers*
10 East 53rd Street
New York, NY 10022
Fax: (212) 207-7654

Library of Congress Control Number: 2011925976
ISBN 978-0-06-200839-8

Book design by Iris Shih

Printed in the United States of America
First Printing, 2011

I haven't had a quiet life. I've lived dangerously. Sometimes disaster has come at me like a train. There have been times when I've almost drunk myself to death. I've been in situations where I was perilously close to killing myself. I've almost died several times. Yet some instinct, some inner force, has always saved me, dragging me back just as the train whooshed past.

—*Elizabeth Taylor*

INTRODUCTION

B road. Dame. Home-wrecker. The most beautiful woman in the world: It was never easy being Elizabeth Taylor, international movie star and femme fatale. A woman of seemingly contradictory passions—as extravagant as she was generous, and as gentle as she was poised for battle—Elizabeth was often misunderstood by her adoring audience, her family, and even, at times, by herself. Her outsize flair for living brought her to the brink of disaster time and time again as she tested the outer limits of her indulgences. Nothing, it seemed, from expensive jewelry to torrid love affairs, could satiate Elizabeth's inner desires. It was only later in life, with her dedicated charity work, that Elizabeth found the peace and stability she sought so desperately.

But who was Elizabeth Taylor? On her own, away from the glare of the paparazzi, the adoring fans, and the many men who loved her, what made Elizabeth Taylor's heart skip a beat? What inspired her sense of glamour, her steely inner core? To understand the elements that made Elizabeth tick, one must go back to her childhood. Her unique upbringing not only helped shape the woman she became, but also forecasted her future as one of Hollywood's most talented stars and uncompromising beauties.

Born in England in 1932 to a well-to-do American family with strong connections to the British upper class, Elizabeth was blessed with a beauty that made people stop and stare. Her mother, Sara, recognized Elizabeth's alluring qualities and downplayed them, if only to emphasize the importance of personality and willpower over physical attributes. It was not until the Taylor family moved to Hollywood that Sara, a former stage actress, understood that Elizabeth's beauty was a powerful calling card, one that gave the family a valuable entrée into the industry's top-level studios and social circles. Sara dedicated her full attention to Elizabeth, priming her for a career in which she herself had achieved only modest success. Elizabeth learned, at an incredibly early age, that perfection in performance meant everything. She endured her mother's strict training as preparation for a life of greatness and reluctantly accepted the fact that there was little or no margin for error. The rebellious nature and wicked tongue that would later come to define Elizabeth Taylor may have been a reaction to the intense scrutiny she suffered as a child. It seemed that everyone—from her perfectionist mother to the cadre of studio execs, agents, and audiences—were waiting and watching for Elizabeth to enter the full bloom of profitable womanhood. If there was ever a need to rebel, Elizabeth Taylor certainly had more than her share of reasons.

By the time she was twelve years old, Elizabeth boasted an impressive resumé, having starred in *Lassie Come Home* and *National Velvet*. By the time she reached fifteen, she was an established star and, as she took on more adult roles, her costars were no longer dogs and horses, but some of Hollywood's most desirable leading men. In 1956, she starred opposite Rock Hudson and James Dean in *Giant*. That role firmly cemented her position as one of Hollywood's reigning actresses, and the hits that followed came in short order: *Cat on a Hot Tin Roof* (1958); *Suddenly, Last Summer* (1959); *BUtterfield 8* (1960); and *Cleopatra* (1963). It was on the set of *Cleopatra* that Elizabeth met her greatest love, Richard Burton.

Elizabeth and Richard ruled over Hollywood for fifteen years, predecessors to the Brangelina and TomKat hysteria that sells the tabloids today. Elizabeth's whirlwind affair with Burton defined scandal, captured the world's attention and imagination, and brought condemnation from the Vatican. Their relationship was punctuated by every kind of excess imaginable, from booze to brawls to total sexual abandon. It was the kind of love Elizabeth craved. Full of larger-than-life highs and profoundly crippling lows, the relationship clearly wasn't perfect, yet that was part of its appeal. Having spent her whole life in the public eye, Elizabeth, at last, felt free. She followed her own rules and did what she pleased, relishing in complete ownership of her life. Though her health paid the price for her having lived so extravagantly for so long, she achieved what few among us ever do: the ability to experience everything life has to offer. In *Cat on a Hot Tin Roof*, Big Daddy Pollitt says, "I've got the guts to die. What I want to know is, have you got the guts to live?" As if taking a cue from these lines, Elizabeth Taylor answers yes, again and again.

A fiercely private person despite her dramatic public outbursts, Elizabeth preferred to simply get down to the business of living her life instead of talking about it. Still, over her lifetime she imparted several gems of wit and wisdom that covered every subject: sex and scandal, beauty and humility, the importance of having a sense of humor, and the truth about dying. As a woman who'd been through it all, she served as a model for living an inspired life and gave millions of women permission to follow their passions, even when conventional wisdom told them not to.

Here, then, is Elizabeth, uncensored, exactly as she would have wanted it.

I think I was
probably born
a ham.

CHILDHOOD

efore she became one of the most legendary actresses of Hollywood's golden age, Elizabeth was just like any other girl...with violet eyes.

Although both of her parents, Francis Lenn Taylor and Sara Viola Warmbrodt, were from the American Midwest, Elizabeth Rosemond Taylor was born in a district of London called Hampstead, on February 27, 1932. The Taylors, including Elizabeth and her older brother, Howard, were comfortable in this semirural pocket of London's northern edge. Francis was an art dealer, who had left the United States to start a gallery in London;

her mother, Sara, was a former actress, who gave up her career when she married Francis.

Although the Taylors had strong connections to the theatre and art worlds, their approach to child-rearing was anything but bohemian. The Taylors were disciplinarians, emphasizing proper appearance and manners. For Elizabeth, this strict upbringing tempered her naturally precocious personality. When she did something wrong, she was "sent to Coventry"—a form of British punishment whereby parents ostracized their disobedient children by not speaking to them. Ignoring Elizabeth was one way of wrestling with—or perhaps encouraging—her rebellious nature. "Of course," Alexander Walker observes in his biography of Elizabeth, "in those days, it didn't cost a film company millions to ignore Elizabeth Taylor." Despite her parents' attempts to keep their daughter from getting too much attention, it wasn't long before Elizabeth found a wider audience.

When Elizabeth was four years old, she, along with several other children, performed at a benefit dance recital for the Duchess of York (the wife of George VI and the future queen mother) and her two daughters, the future Queen Elizabeth II and Princess Margaret, at the Hippodrome, a theatre in London. At curtain call, Elizabeth, dressed as a butterfly, curtsied to the royal party—and continued fluttering around the stage until her mother was finally forced to retrieve her. As Sara declared later, "I knew from the benefit recital that Elizabeth had inherited a certain amount of 'ham.'" The incident became a part of the myth—the genesis story—of Elizabeth Taylor, movie star. At the very least, this childhood anecdote foretold her future as an actress who was never shy at demanding attention—both in her public and private life—and who was able to hold an audience captive, on screen and off.

Until she was seven, Elizabeth lived in England, where she loved to escape from her parents' strict household by exploring the wild countryside of her godfather's estate in Kent on horseback. When World War II broke out, the Taylors returned to the United States, and settled in Los Angeles. Little did Elizabeth know that Hollywood would quickly subsume the idyllic years of her childhood. This new country, as foreign to her as it was exhilarating, forever changed her life, destroying any real chance she had for leading a quiet, normal existence.

Page 12: Elizabeth, circa 1944.

On life before acting

My happiest moments as a child were riding my Newfoundland pony, Betty, in the woods on 3,000 acres of my godfather's estate near the village of Cranbrook.

Those years before I started acting were truly happy.

Elizabeth with her brother,
Howard, and mother,
Sara, circa 1937.

On staying in England

Probably if there hadn't been a World War II, I would have been a debutante, lived in England, and married someone very secure and staid. I never would have become an actress. I would have had as many children as I could physically have had.

Had I been raised in England, my life would have been completely different. Because [my family] settled in Los Angeles, I became a movie star. It was not a normal life, of course. The demands, particularly on the emotional level, were killing.

On being a child star

My [childhood] was overscheduled and overdisciplined.

Looking back I can see that, between the demands of the studio and my parents' strict discipline, it was an impossible way to grow up. But it did make me tough.

Working at age nine is not a childhood.

From the age of nine I began to see
myself as two separate people: Elizabeth
Taylor the person, and Elizabeth Taylor
the commodity. I saw the difference
between my image and my real self.
Sometimes [as a child] when I was
out riding, I would pretend to be part
of a fantasy high school or campus
scene, but a few hours later I would
be back on the set creating the public
Elizabeth Taylor.

Ever since I'd been ten, I'd been a child star with no privacy.

Looking back at myself as a child, I can recognize my precociousness. There was something inside me that wasn't childlike.... I was unusually mature. Given my life, how could I not have been? I grew up surrounded by adults and had adult responsibilities.

Elizabeth and her mother, Sara, 1947.

On growing up on screen

At barely
seventeen,
I grew up
for all America
to see.

Elizabeth with her
parents, circa 1950.

Some of my best leading men have been dogs and horses.

ACTING

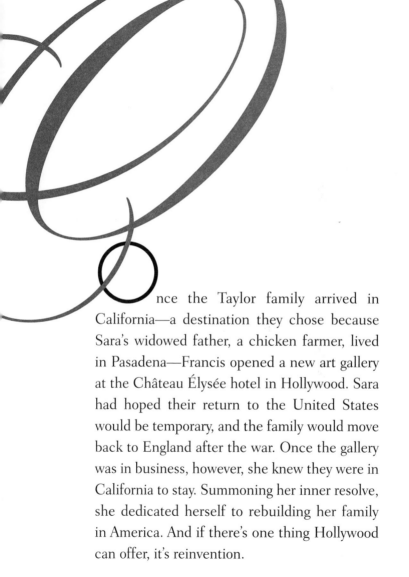

nce the Taylor family arrived in California—a destination they chose because Sara's widowed father, a chicken farmer, lived in Pasadena—Francis opened a new art gallery at the Château Élysée hotel in Hollywood. Sara had hoped their return to the United States would be temporary, and the family would move back to England after the war. Once the gallery was in business, however, she knew they were in California to stay. Summoning her inner resolve, she dedicated herself to rebuilding her family in America. And if there's one thing Hollywood can offer, it's reinvention.

The Taylors soon moved from their temporary home in Pasadena to the Pacific Palisades. There, the Taylors' neighbors included many celebrities—among them, Darryl F. Zanuck, head of Twentieth-Century Fox, and actress Norma Shearer—and young Elizabeth quickly caught their attention. Friends suggested that the Taylors have Elizabeth screen-tested for the role of Vivien Leigh's daughter in the upcoming *Gone with the Wind*. What Elizabeth lacked in dramatic talent—at least at the time—she more than made up for with a gorgeous face that, even at a young age, Hollywood A-listers knew the camera would love. It didn't take long for MGM execs, referred by friends in the business, to come knocking.

Upon seeing her mile-long gaze, Louis B. Mayer reportedly snapped, "Sign her up, sign her up. What are you waiting for?" And so began Elizabeth's perilously long and meandering relationship with the Hollywood studios, as she moved back and forth between heavyweights MGM and Universal for a long list of films that included *There's One Born Every Minute*, *Lassie Come Home*, *Jane Eyre*, and *The White Cliffs of Dover* (her roles in the latter two were uncredited). Her studio relationships may have kept her bound to tight contracts and grueling, regimented filming and schooling schedules, yet MGM and Universal delivered the world to her on a plate—all before the age of eleven. No wonder Elizabeth had mixed feelings about it all, saying in her later years, "I never wanted a career; it was forced on me."

In 1944, Elizabeth's fame skyrocketed when she starred in *National Velvet*. Not only did the film make her a household name, but it was a harbinger of the intense sensuality that Elizabeth would later deliver both on screen, as her public persona, and to an extent as a wife. Speaking about King Charles, the horse that plays The Pie in the film, Elizabeth said, "The [studio was] afraid for me to ride him. But he loves me....You don't have to worry about King....You just leave everything up to him. I think that he likes to know that I leave it to him—that he's the boss and I love him." She expressed similar sentiments about love and the sense of duty for each of her seven husbands—at least at the start of those marriages.

After *National Velvet*, Elizabeth went on to star in a string of films, most of which became classics—*A Place in the Sun*, *Giant*, *Cat on a Hot Tin Roof*, *BUtterfield 8*, and *Suddenly, Last Summer*. Of course, in that mix were some real duds, such as *The Comedians* and *A Little Night Music*. Then there were the huge hits—*Cleopatra* and *Who's Afraid of Virginia Woolf?*, the two films that made Elizabeth a living legend. In the latter, she gave what many consider to be the performance of a lifetime, for which she won an Academy Award for Best Actress. The former was notorious for its extraordinary length and expensive production, and the part it played in her internationally scandalous love affair with Richard Burton. As the love of her life, he was the only man capable of matching her passions. Their romance was a fifteen-year odyssey (if one counts the years encompassing their affair and marriages, but twenty-four, if one counts the years until Burton's death) that ignited the silver screen and fascinated audiences the world over. Their relationship became one of the most defining and tumultuous of the twentieth century.

Page 30: Elizabeth in *Cleopatra*, 1963.

On overcoming shyness

I was constricted by shyness—I still am—and acting meant I could be at least behind someone else's façade.

Everything makes me nervous, except making films.

Elizabeth in *Courage of Lassie*, 1946.

On talent

I don't presume to be a great actress.
I presume to be an effective actress.

On career ambivalence

I never cared whether or not I was
an actress, especially when I was a
very little girl.

Much of my life I've hated acting.

On the difference between being an actress and a movie star

What I would really like is to be good enough [at acting] for people to think of me as an actress, not a movie star. But it is very difficult once you have become part of the public domain to be taken seriously. Part of me is sorry that I became a public utility.

On the importance of being selective later in her career

By not being consumed by ambition, I can wait for the films I really want to do.

On film acting

I think film acting can be an art, and certainly the camera can move in and grab hold of your mind—so the emotion has got to be there behind your eyes, behind your heart.

Page 40: Spencer Tracy and Elizabeth in *Father of the Bride*, 1950.

On her roles

At least once a year I play a has-been actress…I'm a great success at playing has-beens.

The first time I was asked to do any real acting was *A Place in the Sun*.

On an actor's intuition

Whatever it is I may have in acting— that part of me is minuscule—it's not technique. It's instinct and a certain ability to concentrate.

On her favorite leading men

RICHARD BURTON

I'm just a broad, but Richard
is a great actor.

Richard was magnificent in every sense
of the word…and in everything he did.
He was magnificent on the stage, magnificent in film, he was magnificent at
making love…at least to me.

Montgomery Clift

As far as I'm concerned, he introduced a new dimension to screen acting.

Only two actors I know, Monty [Clift] and Richard [Burton], give to the degree that it's almost a physical thing, like an umbilical cord, an electricity that goes back and forth.

The most gorgeous thing
in the world and easily
one of the best actors.

Elizabeth and
Montgomery Clift in
A Place in the Sun, 1951.

James Dean, Elizabeth, and Rock Hudson on the set of *Giant*, 1956.

Though we were linked romantically by the media, I sensed from the beginning that Monty was torn between what he thought he should be and what he actually was.

CLARK GABLE

He was the epitome of a movie star—so romantic, such bearing, such friendliness.

ROCK HUDSON

He was one of the most important people in my life. He was my closest friend.

Roddy McDowall

[He] is really the perfect friend.

Spencer Tracy

He had a stillness, a quietness about him that spoke more than volumes, and it just was mesmerizing.

John Wayne

He is as tough as an old nut and as soft as a yellow ribbon.

Elizabeth and Roddy
McDowall at the
Egyptian Theatre,
Hollywood, 1949.

On success

Success is a great deodorant. It takes away all your past smells.

Power is being able to do what you want to do.

"I want it all quickly 'cause I don't want God to stop and think and wonder if I'm getting more than my share."

—As Velvet Brown, *National Velvet*, 1944

On the public

The public puts you up on a pedestal and then they wait like vultures to tear you down.

The
day
came,
of
course,
when
I
got
a
bit
famous.

Elizabeth in
BUtterfield 8, 1960.

The public seems to revel in the imperfections of the famous, the heroes, and to want to be in a position of attacking—which I guess makes them feel a little bit superior. So I would have delighted lots of fans throughout the world. If anybody has given them an opportunity to feel superior, I have.

Why couldn't they let me grow up like
Suzy Smith with a house in the suburbs,
a husband who takes the 8:10, and
three fat, saucy kids?

On the difference between her public responsibility and her private life

I owe the public who pays to see me
on the screen the best performance
I can give. As to how I live my personal
life, my responsibility is to the people
directly involved with me.

On her films

NATIONAL VELVET

As a child I adored being in films, just as long as there was an animal in them.

National Velvet was really me.

I worked harder on that film than on any other movie in my life.

Mickey Rooney and
Elizabeth in *National
Velvet*, 1944.

"You know what I feel like? I feel all the time like a cat on a hot tin roof."

—As Maggie, *Cat on a Hot Tin Roof*, 1958

CLEOPATRA

I really don't remember much about *Cleopatra*. There were a lot of other things going on.

After my last shot, there was a curiously sad sort of aching, empty feeling—but such astronomical relief. It was finally over. It was like a disease, shooting that film—an illness one had a very difficult time recuperating from.

On being paid one million dollars for *Cleopatra*

That's an idiotic amount to be paid,
but when I was growing up, the studio
always made me feel like so much meat
on the hook. Nowadays, when I can be
cool about a million dollars, I feel like a
nice big steak.

If someone's dumb enough to offer
me a million dollars to make a picture,
I'm certainly not dumb enough to turn
it down.

THE SANDPIPER

We're [Richard Burton and Elizabeth] supposed to play two people in love, and I must say, when we look at each other, it's like our eyes have fingers and they grab ahold.

WHO'S AFRAID OF VIRGINIA WOOLF?

That [film] was fun. It was very cathartic, too, because we [Richard Burton and Elizabeth] would get all our shouting and bawling out on the set and go home and cuddle.

Richard [Burton] and I went on the Drinking Man's Diet after we made *Who's Afraid of Virginia Woolf?* It worked for awhile, and then we dropped the "diet" and just continued drinking. I can't think of a program worse for the liver.

I've never had a better time in my life.

In the years since [Richard Burton's] death, I had avoided watching his movies because it was too painful.... I couldn't hide forever and started watching [*Who's Afraid of Virginia Woolf?*]. As the movie progressed, I was overcome with such a sense of joy and pride. We did something okay, something we'll always have...how lucky I was to have been a part of it....God, we were good together.

Pages 66–67: Elizabeth and Richard Burton in *Who's Afraid of Virginia Woolf?*, 1966.

I had a character to grab ahold of and sink my nails into. [The script] provided wonderful words to wrap your lips around.

Richard and I would be out with friends and I'd hear myself saying to him, "For Chrissakes, shut up. I'm not finished talking." And then the next morning, I would think, "That wasn't me, it was Martha." I had to fight to regain myself.

Martha
completely took
me over.

"I'm loud and I'm vulgar, and I wear the pants in the house because somebody's got to, but I am not a monster. I'm not."

—As Martha, *Who's Afraid of Virginia Woolf?*, 1966

I have totally divorced myself from Martha so when I'm doing Martha, I completely forget anything else I've ever done, or ever was, or ever will be. It's almost like a split personality kind of thing.... I can turn Martha on now. It's the easiest role I've ever played. It's difficult playing yourself. And Martha is so remote from me.

To director Mike Nichols on the set of *Who's Afraid of Virginia Woolf?*

I can't *act* until you say "action."

On accepting her Academy Award for Best Actress for BUtterfield 8

I don't really know how to express my gratitude for this and for everything. All I can say is thank you, thank you with all of my heart.

When I've fallen in love, it's always been the marrying kind of love.

MARRIAGE

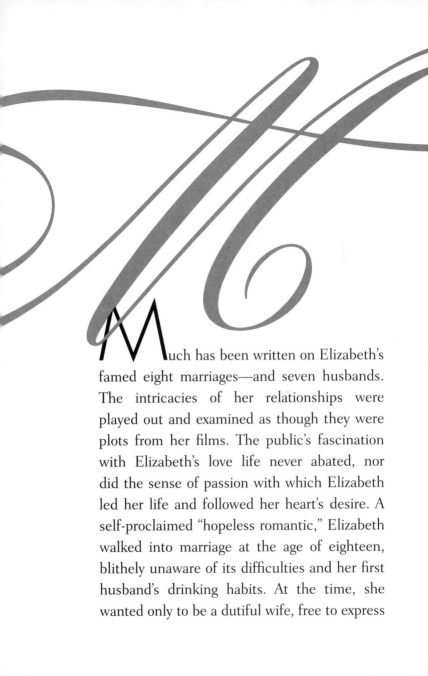

Much has been written on Elizabeth's famed eight marriages—and seven husbands. The intricacies of her relationships were played out and examined as though they were plots from her films. The public's fascination with Elizabeth's love life never abated, nor did the sense of passion with which Elizabeth led her life and followed her heart's desire. A self-proclaimed "hopeless romantic," Elizabeth walked into marriage at the age of eighteen, blithely unaware of its difficulties and her first husband's drinking habits. At the time, she wanted only to be a dutiful wife, free to express her newfound sensuality. In truth, given her unusual adolescence, she had little preparation for understanding the rigors of normal courtship, relationships, and marriage.

An idyllic pairing on paper—Conrad "Nicky" Hilton, heir to the Hilton Hotel fortune, and she, one of the most beautiful, sought-after stars in Hollywood—the couple's marriage was ill-fated, lasting a mere seven months. Elizabeth returned from their honeymoon cruise physically, emotionally, and mentally bruised—Hilton was a cruel drunk. Elizabeth absolved their union as quickly as it had been formed.

In the summer of 1951, almost six months after divorcing Hilton, Elizabeth met her second husband, British actor Michael Wilding, during the filming of *Ivanhoe*. Wilding, married at the time, had been living apart from his wife, actress Kay Young. Mild-mannered and twenty years older than Elizabeth, Wilding was a clear

Page 72: Elizabeth in
Suddenly, Last Summer,
1959.

74

departure from Elizabeth's first husband. They, too, married quickly, with twenty-year-old Elizabeth even buying her own sapphire wedding ring—Wilding was broke after an expensive divorce from Young.

During their five years together, Elizabeth would make eight films (including *Ivanhoe*), among them *The Last Time I Saw Paris*, *Raintree County*, and *Giant*. She also gave birth to their two children: Michael Howard Wilding, Jr. and Christopher Edward Wilding. Despite their seemingly amicable life together, the age difference (according to rumor) caused them to stray from the marriage and ultimately drove them apart. They divorced in 1957, with Elizabeth gaining custody of her children. The two remained friends until Wilding's death in July 1979.

Michael Todd, a successful producer-entrepreneur, wooed Elizabeth from the moment he met her. They married two days after her divorce from Michael Wilding was finalized. Todd's flamboyant style, wealth, and energy swept her up into a captivating world that included fine art collections, a whirlwind of activity, and lavish gifts of jewelry. The couple fascinated the public as they jetted all over the globe, with Todd buying Elizabeth extravagant gifts at every turn, including paintings by Degas, Utrillo, and Vuillard, as well as a 29-carat engagement ring. The press called their union "a marriage of equals," because in addition to their propensity for big love, they also loved a big fight. Elizabeth could dish out as good as she got, and the couple often fought in public—a trait that would be repeated to full and dramatic effect with her fifth husband, Richard Burton. The couple fought in public just so, it seemed, they could make up in front of the cameras: it was as if publicity were a form of foreplay.

On March 22, 1958, thirteen months into the marriage and just a few weeks into the shooting of *Cat on a Hot Tin Roof*, Todd was killed in a plane crash on the couple's private plane, the *Lucky Liz*, over New Mexico. Elizabeth was supposed to be onboard, but due to illness decided not to accompany her husband to New York City, where he was to be roasted by the Friars Club. Todd's sudden death devastated her, and although Elizabeth had described being numb during much of the filming of *Cat on a Hot Tin Roof*, the camera revealed an astonishing performance, a portent of the depth of her great talent and her incredible power to concentrate under extreme personal pressure.

After Todd's death, Elizabeth, who felt lost and in desperate need of an anchor, turned from her former Christian Science faith to Todd's faith, Judaism, in which she said she found the strength and guidance she needed to push through her grief. Crooner Eddie Fisher, Todd's friend and protégé, also comforted Elizabeth through this difficult time. Fisher had been Todd's best man at Mike and Elizabeth's wedding, while his wife, Debbie Reynolds, had been Elizabeth's maid of honor. Fisher and Reynolds's marriage—they were known as "America's sweethearts"—quickly dissolved as Fisher fell in love with Elizabeth. As with most of her relationships with men, what began as a friendship with Fisher soon turned sexual.

The public and the media had a field day with the affair. Sympathy for Elizabeth quickly turned to harsh judgment, with hate letters bombarding newspapers and magazines across the country. When Hollywood reporter Hedda Hopper chided the star for breaking up Reynolds and Fisher, Elizabeth famously replied, "Mike is dead and I'm alive!" Though many felt the marriage was inappropriate, it lasted from May 1959 to March 1964.

And then came *Cleopatra*—and Richard Burton. Though the pair had met casually ten years before filming began in 1961, the spark of their romance was ignited the first day on the set. Burton, true to form, arrived with a wicked hangover, and Elizabeth brought a cup of coffee to his lips—his hands were shaking too badly to help himself—to nurse him back to sobriety. Fascinated with Burton's vulnerability, Elizabeth fell for him almost instantly. Burton was power-less in front of Elizabeth's charms—the violet eyes, the décolletage—and managed to flub his lines during filming, a disarming misstep that only further endeared him to Elizabeth. Their affair began almost instantaneously. Despite pleas by their spouses, the Taylor-Burton attraction was too strong, and their love was too intense, for either to walk away. As Elizabeth herself remarked, "Nobody tells me who to love, or not to love, who to be seen with and who not to be seen with." And so began their tumultuous relationship, a whirlwind on-again, off-again cycle of insatiable desire, passionate fights, and true companionship that lasted fifteen years.

The media touched every corner of their lives. Headlines about the couple often knocked more politically relevant news off the front pages. They were stalked incessantly, and the flurry of activity that surrounded them spawned the notion of modern-day paparazzi. Their flamboyant behavior prompted the Vatican to issue a reproach and was denounced by a congresswoman on the floor of the U.S. House of Representatives, but even those responses didn't hinder their affair.

Their romance and resulting two marriages fascinated everyone and redefined love. In the Taylor-Burton world, love wasn't a precious thing, but a breathing entity, forever to be negotiated and handled with a sense of abandonment. In every capacity, their relationship was larger-than-life—from the endless supply of champagne and liquor to their lovemaking, from Burton's extravagant gifts, like the Krupp Diamond, to their numerous luxurious homes.

Unfortunately, it was only a matter of time before their lavish lifestyle consumed Elizabeth and Richard. Much like their characters in *Who's Afraid of Virginia Woolf?*, their wanton drinking and playful fighting turned dark, revealing hidden demons neither one could fully shake, least of all in each other's company. In 1974, ten years after their marriage, they divorced, only to remarry in 1975, and then divorce for good in 1976. But Elizabeth remained very much in Burton's grip, their relationship indelibly imprinted on her psyche, even after his death in 1984. Burton was an impossible act to follow, although two men tried—John Warner, a U.S. senator from Virginia, and Larry Fortensky.

The very wealthy Warner offered Elizabeth the lavish lifestyle to which she had grown so accustomed, and since she was largely indifferent to her film career at this time, the life of a housewife—something that she had always feigned interest in—appealed to her. She soon discovered, however, that being a senator's wife wasn't for her; she was bored and lonely, lost without a sense of purpose or direction. Married in 1976, shortly after her divorce from Burton, the couple divorced in November 1982, but remained on good terms, so good, in fact, that when Elizabeth was hospitalized in 1990 with pneumonia, Warner sent his chef on his private airplane to serve Elizabeth one of her favorite meals: fried chicken and mashed potatoes.

Following her divorce from Warner, Elizabeth remained unmarried for nearly a decade, the longest stretch of her adult life between husbands. She filled most of that time with charity work for AIDS research and by starting her perfume brands. But she continued to struggle with alcohol and drug abuse and was admitted to the Betty Ford Clinic twice, first in 1983 for drug and alcohol addiction, and again in 1988 for prescription pill abuse. During her second rehab stay, she met her eighth husband, construction worker Larry Fortensky. What was the attraction? Companionship—and the help they gave each other to face their common problems. They married in October 1991, but the relationship ended in divorce in October 1996.

Remarkably, in spite of seven divorces, Elizabeth and her former husbands said little about the marriages publicly, although much has been written about these relationships by others. Elizabeth's own comments regarding her marriages tended to be noncommittal or factual, and in some cases, almost affectionate. Although she was occasionally defensive about her numerous marriages, she was always the romantic, saying at one point, "I've only slept with men I've been married to. How many women can make that claim?"

My mother says
I didn't open my
eyes for eight days
after I was born,
but when I did, the
first thing I saw
was an engagement
ring. I was hooked.

On her love of older men

I didn't date until I was about sixteen—and then it was with boys of twenty-three.

On marrying at eighteen

I was too inexperienced to know the right man from the wrong.

I thought marriage was a cottage with a white picket fence and roses climbing over it....I was unprepared for that world.

On marital love

I was, I'm afraid, wildly infatuated
with love.

If you hear of me getting married
[again], slap me!

On marital values

I have an old-fashioned sense of a wife's
obligations and always have been the
malleable one in marital situations.

My sense of right and wrong makes it very difficult for me to have an affair. I have to be really in love in order to sleep with a man, and when I'm really in love, I want to be married.

The irony is that the morality I learned at home required marriage; I couldn't just have an affair. So I got married all those times, and now I'm accused of being a scarlet woman. I guess I never gave myself the time to find out whether a thing was love or infatuation. I always chose to think I was in love.

On marriage itself

Marriage is a great institution.

It's an addiction I couldn't give up.

It's funny how any announcement
I make turns into a marriage.

I don't pretend to be an ordinary
housewife.

On womanhood and sexuality

[Marriage] seemed the only way I could experience life for myself and, perhaps most important of all, discover my own sexuality.

I really thought in those days that just because I became a Mrs. instead of a Miss, just because I hit twenty-one, something would automatically happen to me inside. . . . I don't think I even analyzed whether it was maturity I wanted—probably just the glamour of being a woman.

I am sorry I did not fully understand
the reasons driving me into early
matrimony. At the time I just knew I
ached to become a real woman, a wife.

I like being a woman and I think sex is
absolutely gorgeous.

On being a hopeless romantic

I was then and am now an incurable
romantic.

On men

I believe in the difference between men and women. In fact, I embrace the difference.

I truly believe I can be content only with a man who's a bit crazy.

I suppose when they reach a certain age, some men are afraid to grow up. It seems the older men get, the younger their wives get.

On sex appeal

I can tell you what I think is sexy in a man. It has to do with warmth, a personal givingness, not self-awareness.

If my husband thinks I'm sexy, that's good enough for me.

On being a wife

I am a very committed wife. And I should be committed, too—for being married so many times.

I love being me, not Elizabeth Taylor,
but Richard Burton's wife.

On divorce

I know it's incongruous for me to say it,
but I don't believe in divorce.

"I swear to God, George, if you even
existed, I'd divorce you."

—As Martha, *Who's Afraid of
Virginia Woolf?*, 1966

On her husbands

I never planned to acquire a lot of jewels or a lot of husbands.

The Many Marriages of Elizabeth Taylor

All of Elizabeth's marriages ended in divorce, except for the one to Michael Todd, which left her a widow.

Conrad "Nicky" Hilton
May 6, 1950–January 29, 1951

Michael Wilding
February 21, 1952–January 31, 1957

Michael Todd
February 2, 1957–March 22, 1958

Eddie Fisher
May 12, 1959–March 6, 1964

Richard Burton
March 15, 1964–June 26, 1974

October 10, 1975–August 1, 1976

John Warner
December 4, 1976–November 7, 1982

Larry Fortensky
October 6, 1991–October 31, 1996

Nicky Hilton

When I met Nicky Hilton, I was ripe
to get married. Dazzled by his charm
and apparent sophistication, driven
by feelings that could not be indulged
outside of marriage, desperate to live a
life independent of my parents and the
studio, I closed my eyes to any problem
and walked radiantly down the aisle.

On their divorce
I fell off my pink cloud with a thud.

On not asking Hilton
for alimony
I don't need a prize for failing.

Michael Wilding

I just want to be with Michael and be his wife. He enjoys sitting at home, smoking a pipe, reading, painting. And that's what I intend on doing—except smoking a pipe.

He restored all sanity [and] represented tranquillity, security, maturity—all the things I needed.

Page 96: Nicky Hilton and Elizabeth, circa 1950. Opposite: Elizabeth and Michael Wilding, circa 1952.

I'm afraid in those last few years I gave him a rather rough time. Sort of hen-pecked him and probably wasn't mature enough for him. It wasn't that we had anything to fight over.

Michael Todd

I love him madly. Why do I love him so much? Because the first time he made love to me, I think my heart stopped beating.

Sure, Mike and I fight. But some people just can't tell a fight from a family frolic.

We scream at each other all the time, using those Latin gestures. Actually neither of us is inhibited, so we speak frankly to each other.... We have more fun fighting than most people do just making love.

It's nice to be married to someone with a brain.

He knew how much I loved paintings. He loved paintings, too, but instead of buying himself the paintings, he'd buy them for me.

He had a joy, a vitality that was flamboyant.

Elizabeth and
Michael Todd, 1956.

Eddie Fisher

I'm not taking anything away from Debbie [Reynolds], because she never really had it.

Maybe with Eddie I was trying to see if I was alive or dead.

[Our marriage] was clearly a mistake, and I don't want to hurt Eddie. I've done too much of that already.

Elizabeth and Eddie Fisher on the set of *Suddenly, Last Summer*, 1959.

Richard Burton

ON THEIR ATTRACTION

Richard and I had incredible chemistry together. We couldn't get enough of each other.

Even with paparazzi hanging out of the trees and hearing them tramping over the rooftops above us, even with all that going on, we could make love, and play Scrabble, and spell out naughty words for each other, and the game would never be finished. When you get aroused playing Scrabble, that's love, baby.

We were like magnets, alternately pulling toward each other and, inexorably,
pushing away.

We like to say that we were on the same
beam so much that we triggered each
other off.

Imagine having Richard Burton's voice
in your ear while you are making love. It
drowned out the troubles, the sorrows,
everything just melted away.

Richard is a very sexy man. He's got that sort of jungle essence that one can sense.

I was the happy recipient of a man who knew how to please a woman. Being unfaithful to Richard was as impossible as not being in love with him.

On their affair

We tried to stay away from each other. We were too aware of the pain we were causing others to stay together. But it is a hard thing to do, to run away from your fate. When you are in love and lust like that, you just grab it with both hands and ride out the storm.

Ah well, another day, another drama.

To tell you the truth, I haven't kept track of my so-called public image. I know that, in the American press, I must get *shticklech*, which is a good Jewish word for needles right below the heart.... [But] why get a heart attack over [such press]? I suppose [the public] rather regards me as a scarlet woman. I guess I seem so scarlet I'm almost purple.

You find out who your real friends are
when you're involved in a scandal.

Cleopatra: Antony, what has happened?
Antony: To me? You have happened to me.

—*Cleopatra*, 1963

I did not want to be another notch
on his belt.

On her love for Burton

It was so intense. There is something very mystic about all Welsh people. And that sense of poetry and wildness was where I had always wanted to be. I had wanted to be free, running in the rain on the grass, and just nothing to tether me. I just wanted to go.

Pages 112–113:
Richard Burton and
Elizabeth, 1965.

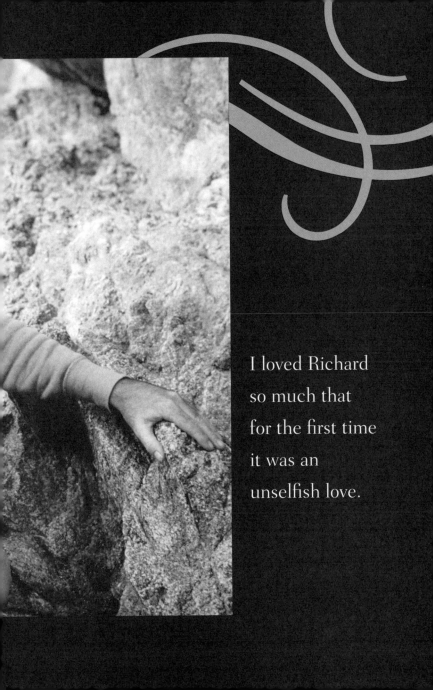

I loved Richard
so much that
for the first time
it was an
unselfish love.

I love Richard Burton with every
fiber of my soul, but we can't
be together. Maybe we loved each
other too much.... Pray for us.

It seems curious that our society today
finds illicit love more attractive than
married love. Our love is married love
now. But there is still a suggestion,
I suppose, of rampant sex on the wild.

To have found, through trial and error,
a tranquillity in proud subordination is
so beautiful.

I don't ever want to be that much
in love ever again.

ON THEIR FIGHTS

Richard loses his temper with true
enjoyment. It's beautiful to watch. Our
fights are delightful screaming matches,
and Richard is rather like a small atom
bomb going off.

Our bed was where the fighting stopped.

ON THEIR LIFE TOGETHER

Creating a life with him was far more interesting than interpreting somebody else's life on screen, but then I've always lived my life with too much relish to be a mere interpreter of dreams.

With Richard Burton, I was living my own fabulous, passionate fantasy.

My favorite time is when we're alone at night, giggling and talking about books, world events, poetry, the children, when we first met, daydreams, real dreams.

What can I say about my life with
Richard Burton other than it was full
of transcendent joy?

Sometimes his joy was perverse, and
he would become dark.

I'm pretty enough. My best feature
is my gray hairs. I have them all named;
they're all called Burton.

I wouldn't give up one minute of my time with Richard Burton.

On their excessive lifestyle

Our credo might have been "Eat, drink, and be merry, for tomorrow we have to report to work."

Richard and I lived life to the fullest, but we also paid our dues.

On the possibility of their reconciliation

It was inevitable that we would be married again.

In my heart, I will always believe we would have been married a third and final time…from those first moments in Rome we were always madly and powerfully in love. We had more time, but not enough.

John Warner

I thought we would get married, live
on the farm, raise horses.... Shit, man.
It was going to be my dream.

I think they [Washington, D.C.
insiders] thought I was a freak, which
is probably true.

I tried very hard to make it work and
I love John; he's a wonderful man and a
wonderful politician...there just wasn't
room in his life for me, for family.

If you're a politician's wife and don't have your own role, there is nothing for you to do but be supportive. I really had to keep my mouth shut.

The U.S. Senate is a very hard mistress to fight.

ON HER WEIGHT GAIN
It's a happy fat. I eat because I'm so happy.

Page 120: John Warner and Elizabeth, 1978.

Larry Fortensky

[It] may not look like we had a lot in common, but he was a very sweet, gentle man who wanted to experience life, who wanted to go out and taste what it was like out there; he'd never left California.

I was so proud when he kept on
working—and then it just all started
to change.

He just really couldn't kind of go with it.
I don't want to blame him. We just
stopped communicating.

Larry Fortensky and
Elizabeth, 1991.

I've never felt
so important in
all my life.
I've never felt
so beautiful.

IV

MOTHERHOOD

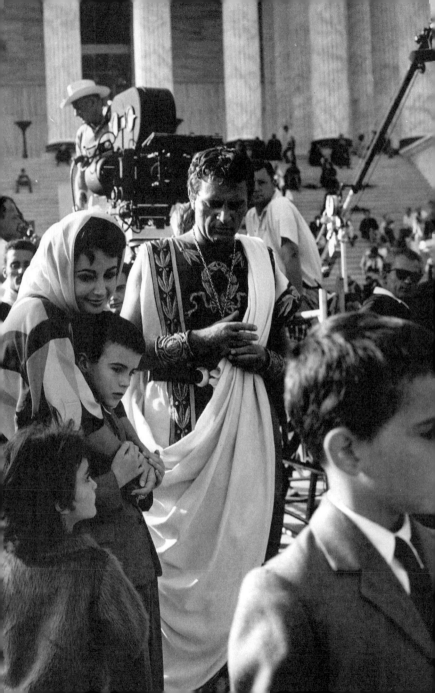

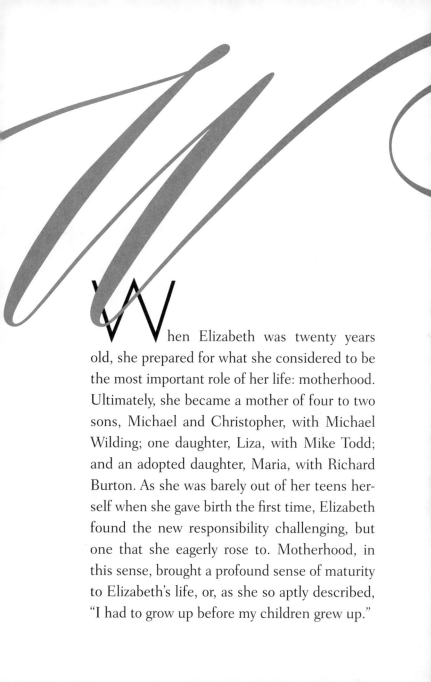

When Elizabeth was twenty years old, she prepared for what she considered to be the most important role of her life: motherhood. Ultimately, she became a mother of four to two sons, Michael and Christopher, with Michael Wilding; one daughter, Liza, with Mike Todd; and an adopted daughter, Maria, with Richard Burton. As she was barely out of her teens herself when she gave birth the first time, Elizabeth found the new responsibility challenging, but one that she eagerly rose to. Motherhood, in this sense, brought a profound sense of maturity to Elizabeth's life, or, as she so aptly described, "I had to grow up before my children grew up."

Elizabeth's own childhood had been a rocky one. Beyond the strict tenets and schedules set by the Hollywood studios, Elizabeth was forced to navigate the tough love doled out by her domineering parents. Whatever goodness Elizabeth drew from her own childhood, she sought to bring into the lives of her own children.

She was determined to protect her private life and made no apologies for her personal travails to the public. There were moments, though, when her children were caught in the crossfire of the paparazzi's lenses or became the subject of tabloid gossip. Of course, being a film icon came with its own set of intricate challenges that directly affected her children's lives. The family moved a great deal, shuttling between various on-site location shoots in foreign cities and living abroad like a band of roving gypsies. While seemingly romantic—who wouldn't want to travel the globe?—the instability proved daunting for the children.

And then there were her many marriages, which Elizabeth acknowledged as being emotionally difficult for the children, despite the fact that each of her husbands had genuine affection for her kids, and they for them. Without a doubt, though, they were most fond of and influenced by Richard Burton. Not only did he play a fatherly role in their lives the longest, but, according to Elizabeth, her children thoroughly enjoyed his lively, demonstrative nature.

Ironically, for a woman constantly scrutinized by the media, motherhood gave Elizabeth the one thing she truly craved: a sense of privacy. Playing with her children, taking delight in her grandchildren's accomplishments, and watching her family grow and prosper, Elizabeth had the freedom to simply *be*. In this intimate sphere, she was "Mommy": not the famous movie star but her children's source of comfort and love. And for once that role was enough for her.

Page 128: Richard Burton with Elizabeth and her children on the set of *Cleopatra*, 1963.

On being a mother

I think it's much more important for a woman to be a mother than an actress. I've been an actress for fifteen years. Now I want to be a woman!

Oh, I wish I could completely explain how I feel about having a baby…. Procreation is like the tide, it's like the planets, it's like everything inexplicable. And yet it's so utterly personal.

Believe it or not, to my kids I'm not Elizabeth Taylor at all; I'm not anybody other than "Mommy."

On the impact her life had on her children

Their lives have been up and down. We've lived like gypsies. And…well… there's the obvious—I've been married too many times.

On her love for her children

They make me the proudest of anything that I've ever done in my life.

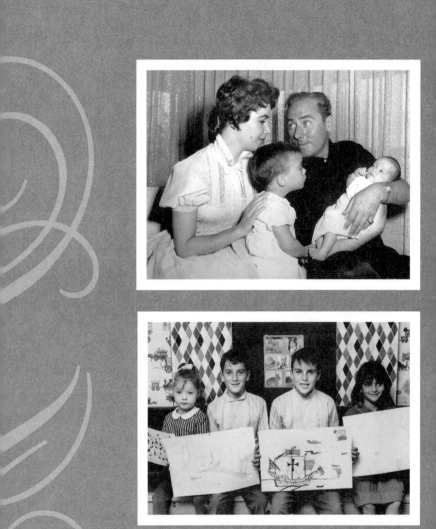

I think all of my children are very remarkable people. Each one is so individual, so different. At the same time they are like me.

I have never felt more alive than when I watched my children delight in something.

Opposite, top: Elizabeth with Michael Wilding and their sons Michael (left) and Christopher (right), 1955. Opposite, bottom: Elizabeth's children, from left to right: Maria Burton, Christopher Wilding, Michael Wilding, Jr., and Liza Todd, 1964. Pages 136–137: Elizabeth and her daughter Liza in England, circa 1970.

Throughout everything,
my children have been the one
consistently bright spot in my life.

My motto
has always been
to be true to
myself, whether
it pleases others
or not.

SELF

As is true for all of us, Elizabeth's experiences shaped her; but unlike for most of us, her experiences were quite unusual and influenced her sense of self in ways that both strengthened her and made her vulnerable. A precocious beauty from birth, she grew into a sensuous woman with appetites that enhanced as well as haunted her throughout her life.

The constant exposure was a double-edged sword for the actress. While the publicity was superb for her career, the world's desire to know the most private details of her life eventually made Elizabeth feel as though she was living

under a microscope. In defense, she developed a keen sense of herself, of what she valued, and of what and whom she loved. Her sense of personal humility also helped defeat the hurt feelings that came with public criticism. At the same time, she believed "in mind over matter and doing anything you set your mind on."

Elizabeth valued her independence and the advantages of power, sometimes to the point of appearing arrogant, which resulted in rumors of her temperamental behavior. Elizabeth's passionate nature often drove her to flaunt convention. She once famously said, "I know I'm vulgar, but would you have me any other way?" That kind of raw honesty—both with herself and with the public—was, and still is, rare, especially among celebrities.

Elizabeth's raucous sense of humor was a healthy partner to her honesty and frankness. Though gorgeous and incredibly feminine, Elizabeth could just as easily have been one of the guys, hoisting glasses of Jack Daniels and peppering salty jokes with enough swear words to make a sailor's head spin. Her most pointed jokes, however, came at her own expense. Turning her jabs inward, she described herself in a number of ways, depending upon the events, the circumstances, and her mood. Never one to shy away from her personal struggles, Elizabeth spoke out about her difficulties with her weight, health, and alcoholism as well as her decision to enter the Betty Ford Clinic for rehabilitation in the 1980s.

Tough yet somewhat philosophical about life, Elizabeth saw in herself an ability to survive, to reach out, and, above all, to enjoy. If life taught her one thing, it was this: "You are who you are. All you can do in this world is help others to be who they are and better themselves and those around them." In 2000, Elizabeth was awarded the DBE, Dame of the British Empire, by Queen Elizabeth II. Although she was thrilled with this honor, in true Taylor fashion she cracked, "I've always been a broad, now I'm a dame."

Page 140: Elizabeth, circa 1960.

On being Elizabeth Taylor

So much to do, so little done,
such things to be.

Even as a child, I insisted on deter-
mining my own fate.

The Elizabeth Taylor who's famous,
the one of celluloid, really has no
depth or meaning to me. It's a totally
superficial working thing, a commodity.

I was always able to sell
Elizabeth Taylor.

People who know me well
call me Elizabeth. I dislike Liz.

No one is going to play Elizabeth Taylor
but Elizabeth Taylor herself.

On acceptance

I find myself much more relaxed
and confident and aware just now.
I don't entirely approve of some of the
things I've done, or am, or have been.
But I'm me. God knows I'm me.

On honesty

Even at my worst, I feel I was true
to myself.

"Truth is the one thing I've never
resisted."

—As Catherine Holly,
Suddenly, Last Summer, 1959

On happiness

Tragedy, mistakes, shame for your mistakes cannot leave you untouched....
And I treat the happiness I have now with great respect, great appreciation, because I know how fragile and precarious it is—how easily it can go.

I am more aware that happiness is a composite total, that it is not some sort of sweet, safe heaven. To mean anything, it must include unhappiness. For me to see this is like being given a whole new world.

Happiness
wasn't
bestowed
on
me;
I
earned
it.

Elizabeth at the 64th
Academy Awards, 1992.

On aspiration

I knew that I wanted more in my life than what I had.

It's not the having, it's the getting.

On integrity

Even as a kid I never sacrificed my personal integrity for my career.

On knowing your limits

Never let yourself think beyond
your means…mental, emotional,
or otherwise.

On rehab

It's like peeling an onion:
you shed layers.

I felt for the first time in my life, since
I was nine, that I wasn't being exploited
by anyone. I was accepted for myself.

For the first time in my life, I shared a room with a woman!

On resilience

Work and the strong inner core I had developed as a child helped keep my optimism, my romanticism, alive.

My physical recovery, like my mental recovery, stems from a sense of strength, not any frantic need for self-improvement.

I'm convinced the inner strength that rescued me from my destructive slide many years later was forged during those early studio years when I was determined always to maintain control over my personal life regardless of studio demons.

Stubbornness, pride—they're not particularly attractive attributes, but they are necessary to keep you alive.

[T]he deaths of so many good friends, terrible illnesses, destructive addictions, broken marriages. All things considered, I'm damned lucky to be alive.

I've been through it all, baby.
I'm Mother Courage. I'll be dragging my sable coat behind me in old age.

Once you're up there on the last rung,
you can only go down. I don't want
to be pushed off. I want to walk down
with all the dignity I can summon—
and not with crutches.

"I catch cold even from weather
forecasts."

—As Helen Ellswirth,
The Last Time I Saw Paris, 1954

On regret

Let's face it—a lot of my life
has lacked dignity.

On owning up to your mistakes

We all have to participate in our own
downfalls, and it doesn't absolve you to
cop a plea by throwing mud on other
people. The one who throws the mud
is always reduced.

Elizabeth on the set
of *Giant*, Marfa,
Texas, 1955.

On the importance of friends

You need supporters, not saboteurs.

On becoming a woman

Although I had been eager to grow up,
I didn't perceive myself as no longer
being a child until I was sixteen. The
turning point was a shooting session
with Philippe Halsman. He was the first
person to make me look at myself as a
woman.... I became intensely aware
of my body.

On being a femme fatale

You might say I'm an escape from diapers and dishwashers—like the boy-meets-girl novelettes. I guess there's that suggestion of the naughty—maybe envy because I've had the honesty to do what some people maybe didn't do at one point in their lives.

Page 161: Elizabeth in a still from *X, Y and Zee*, 1972.

On challenges

I believe people are like rocks formed by the weather. We're formed by experience, by heartache, by grief, by mistakes, by guilt, by shame—all the things that psychiatrists would like to take off your shoulders. But how do you become a full-fledged human being without taking the brunt head-on?

I don't think of myself as beautiful; I never have.

VI

BEAUTY
& AGING

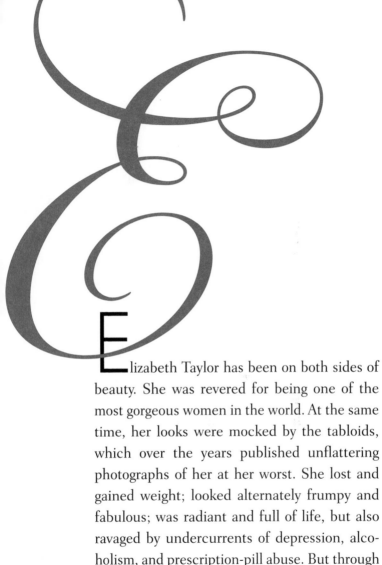

lizabeth Taylor has been on both sides of beauty. She was revered for being one of the most gorgeous women in the world. At the same time, her looks were mocked by the tabloids, which over the years published unflattering photographs of her at her worst. She lost and gained weight; looked alternately frumpy and fabulous; was radiant and full of life, but also ravaged by undercurrents of depression, alcoholism, and prescription-pill abuse. But through all physical extremes, she maintained her sense of authenticity.

As her mother emphasized intellect and artistic talent over looks, Elizabeth grew up unaware of her physical beauty. Only when she arrived in Hollywood did she begin to have an inkling that her attributes were a precious commodity. As her film career grew, Elizabeth graduated from the roles that featured her as an adorable child alongside beloved pets in *National Velvet* and *Lassie Come Home* to a siren holding her own in love scenes with leading men. Her transition to womanhood was carefully guided and monitored by studio executives, who saw her voluptuous figure as an antidote to the waif-thin look that dominated the industry at the time. Here, finally, was a real beauty, a woman who could contend with men.

Elizabeth's response to all the attention was to disassociate from it. As she saw it, her body, the source of her beauty, became Elizabeth Taylor, a product to sell when she needed to. But her physicality never defined her; in fact, her looks were sometimes more of a curse than a blessing. Mike Nichols, the director of *Who's Afraid of Virginia Woolf?*, once asked Elizabeth if she felt trapped by her beauty. Her response: "God, I can't wait for it to go." For Elizabeth, beauty was about having ownership of one's own life, flaws and all. And if there's one thing Elizabeth Taylor owned, it was herself.

She called herself Mother Courage—an apt description. Whatever physical ailments bedeviled her, Elizabeth soldiered on, confident that her inner strength would pull her through. What, then, did she fear of aging? Of death? The whole of Elizabeth's life was based on passion, even pure abandon, of committing herself to the journey at hand, even when that path of self-discovery had been marred by ugly truths and possible destruction. Elizabeth was never in better form than when she'd lost herself and then, miraculously, found and built herself anew. Her warrior's approach to aging was not a wholly graceful one, but it was honest, raw, and utterly admirable.

Page 164: Elizabeth, circa 1950.

On Hollywood's standards of beauty

Growing up in Hollywood never was the glamorous existence you read about in the magazines. Appearance meant everything.

On the industry's waif-thin models

I wish I could be that size, but I can't be. I enjoy food too much. I'm too hedonistic. I enjoy pleasures.

On her weight fluctuations

I'll never try and tell you dieting is fun.

On who she dresses for

Men first. Myself. Then other women.
'Cause you can't please women.
They are horribly critical of each other.
And more so if you're famous. Meow.

On women she finds beautiful

I think Ava Gardner is truly beautiful;
I think my daughter Liza is. I think
Jacqueline Kennedy is a beautiful
woman—tremendous dignity. I am
pretty enough.

On vanity

Today all I see in the mirror every morning is a face that needs washing.

As far as beauty in a woman is concerned, the thing that can kill it is being
too impeccable, too well-nurtured, too
taken care of, so you can feel the vanity
behind it.

Elizabeth in *Ash*
Wednesday, 1973.

On self-image

In overcoming seemingly insurmount-able obstacles, I learned that my oversized body wasn't the biggest barrier to my self-esteem. To regain a healthy sense of self-worth I first had to break down old fears and doubts and anxieties. Only then was I able to reshape my image successfully.

If self-image is based on self and not tied to any role, there is always a sense of anticipation, of moving forward.

In the end, it really only matters what you think of yourself.

There is no greater boost to the self-esteem than to have others acknowledge that you are in control.

The kind of beauty where you're afraid to smile too much is such a bore.

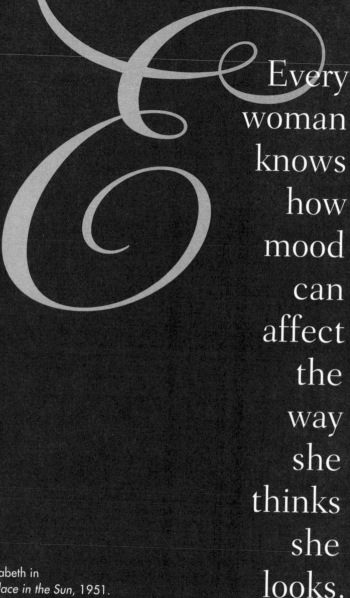

Every woman knows how mood can affect the way she thinks she looks.

Elizabeth in
A Place in the Sun, 1951.

Why shouldn't my outward appearance match all the good feelings inside?

You have to accept yourself for what you are. If what you are includes some gray hairs and a few wrinkles, so what! Remember, self-acceptance is essential to many things.

On keeping perspective

Try not to take yourself too seriously.

Elizabeth at a baby shower for first husband Nicky Hilton's sister, Marilyn, 1950.

On turning forty

Forty isn't the end of the world. It can be the beginning.

On turning fifty-three

I think I'm finally growing up—and about time.

On turning fifty-five

Fifty-five years! I've sure come a long way since *Lassie*.

On the importance of laughter

A belly laugh increases the ability of your immune system to fight infections.

Humor is the only way to stay alive.

On patience

It is strange that the years can teach us patience; that the shorter our time, the greater our capacity for waiting.

On aging gracefully

I never think about growing old;
I barely think about growing up.

Elizabeth in *The Sandpiper*, 1965.

I am sincerely not worried about getting old. Practically all the women I know who were pretty young women became beautiful older women.

As you get older, what you are begins to affect your looks.

I think what age and living and experience do to one's face is beautiful.

On her doctors' prognoses

My body's a real mess. The bone doctors just throw up their hands and say, "Sorry, there's nothing we can do!" Which is so cheery.

On death

I've been too close to death to fear it anymore. I enjoy life far too much to want to die. But I'm certainly not afraid of it. I've been as close as you can get about four times.

I'm not worried about dying. I consult with God, my maker. And I don't have a lot of problems to work out. I'm pretty squared away.

I don't believe our spirits die. I think our spirits are out there, and other people's souls intermingle with ours, and I don't think there is such a thing, like in the movies, the end. I think something continues.

When people say, "She's got everything," I've got one answer—I haven't got tomorrow.

A girl
can always
have more.

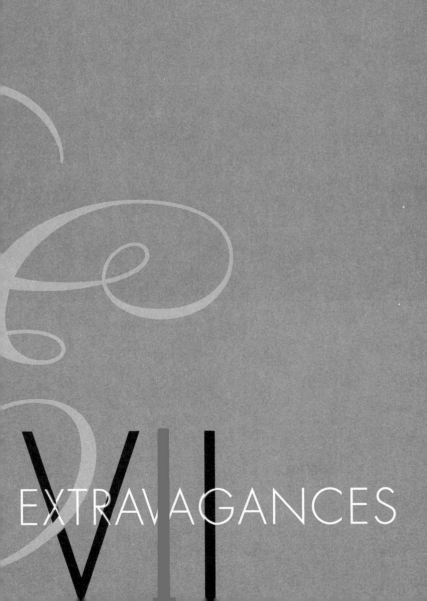

VII

EXTRAVAGANCES

Elizabeth was guided through life by one word, which dictated her love for sex, food and drink, and every luxury imaginable: more. On the one hand, her insatiable appetite came from her realization that life is fleeting, best to enjoy it now. On the other, she was predisposed to a life of extravagance: She grew up with an appreciation of fine art and the trappings that accompanied high-class British society and, later, Hollywood celebrity status.

Just as it had opened doors in England, her father's art gallery gave the Taylors connections to Hollywood's most socially elite and powerful.

Elizabeth witnessed firsthand how a beautiful work of art could seduce powerful men and make them pay attention. She never forgot the lesson and used it in her personal arsenal of seduction tactics, causing men to shower her with gifts that she would later display to dizzying effect. One need only think of the 69.42-carat pear-shaped Cartier Taylor-Burton diamond—a gift from husband to wife, which she famously donned at the 1970 Academy Awards while wearing a one-of-a-kind, low-cut gown designed by Edith Head.

And then, of course, there were her daily extravagances of champagne, caviar, sable coats, yachts, million-dollar houses, and a laundry list of other impulse buys. Glamorous? Fun? Excessive? Yes, yes, and yes. But to Elizabeth, collecting beautiful things was not so much to own them but to luxuriate in them for the moment. In her view, a rare piece—her 33.19-carat Krupp diamond, for example—was a pleasure to behold and touch. To her mind, ownership, like the perfumed scent of a woman, was fleeting and intangible.

When told that Julia Roberts was paid $20 million per picture

I started it.

On her idea of a diet

We're all dieting. That's why we are ordering lima beans, corn on the cob, steak and kidney pie, and mashed potatoes.

On possessions

We [Richard Burton and Elizabeth] get
a great giggle out of all our things. The
yacht, the Rolls, a sable fur coat.

Some people believe it is vulgar to show
their possessions, but we show ours. In
Gstaad, it is fun to look at all the things
we've collected over the years.

On simple luxuries

Fragrance is an incredibly intimate thing. It can evoke very specific thoughts or memories and is a little different for each person who wears it....It's the most accessible luxury.

On frugality

I sort of try to live on a budget.

Diamonds Are a Girl's Best Friend

Elizabeth developed a particular fondness for extravagant gifts early in life. After National Velvet wrapped, MGM gave her the horse that had starred in the movie. How could they not—she claimed to be the only one able to ride him. Her appetite for all things lavish increased as she grew up, and she began to expect tiny (by her definition, that is) tokens from directors and husbands alike. Her happiest marriages, to Todd and Burton, were also the ones in which she received the most lavish gifts.

Elizabeth wearing a Cartier ruby-and-diamond set given to her by Mike Todd, 1958.

Jewelry from Michael Todd

Mike Todd gave Elizabeth extravagant gifts more often than most husbands give flowers. It's hard to imagine how big her collection would have been if his life hadn't been cut short. Some of his memorable offerings:

An antique diamond tiara from 1880, which she wore to the Academy Awards in 1957, the year Todd's film *Around the World in Eighty Days* won Best Picture.

Elizabeth wearing a tiara
from Mike Todd and
Bulgari earrings from
Richard Burton, 1963.

- A Cartier ruby-and-diamond set that included a necklace, earrings, and a bracelet valued at the time at $250,000, given to her when she was pregnant with their daughter Liza.

- A 29.4-carat diamond engagement ring that Elizabeth called her "ice skating rink." Todd joked about the size of the ring, saying that it "was 29 and $7/8$ carats because 30 would have been vulgar."

Jewelry from Richard Burton

Like Todd, Richard Burton used almost any opportunity to don his wife with some truly amazing jewelry. He gave Elizabeth more than thirty highly sought-after pieces, including:

- A number of emerald-and-diamond pieces—a necklace, a pair of earrings, brooches, rings, and bracelets—from Bulgari, or as Elizabeth called it, "Bulgari's nice little shop." The couple often visited Bulgari while filming *Cleopatra* in Rome.

- The Krupp diamond, perhaps her most famous piece, a staggering 33.19-carat gem purchased for $305,000 in 1968.

- The Taj Mahal diamond, which dates from the seventeenth century, on a gold-and-ruby Cartier chain, given to her on her fortieth birthday.

- The La Peregrina pearl, bought by Burton for $37,000 in 1969, and set into a necklace of Cartier diamonds and rubies that Elizabeth designed herself.

The Taylor-Burton diamond, a pear-shaped diamond cut by Harry Winston that weighed an impressive 69.42 carats. Lloyd's of London insured the diamond, which Burton bought for $1,100,000, and stipulated that Elizabeth could only wear the piece in public thirty days a year and in the company of armed guards. In 1978, she sold the diamond to a New York jeweler for $3,000,000 to help fund her then-new husband John Warner's senatorial campaign. She later regretted her decision, saying, "I'm still sick that I sold it."

Elizabeth wearing the Taylor-Burton diamond necklace and the Krupp diamond ring, 1970.

On jewelry

I want to see some rings and things!

Elizabeth: It's the little things
   that count.
Mike Todd: Little diamonds,
   little rubies, little emeralds.

Richard Burton: What are you
   doing, Lumpy?
Elizabeth: Playing with my jewels.

On the Krupp diamond given to her by Richard Burton

> I never stop looking at it, admiring it, not getting over the fact that it's really mine. It's a different sunset every night. It pleasures me.

The Krupp is an extraordinary stone.
It has such life and brilliance when light
shines through it. Size does matter,
but so does the size of the emotion
behind it.

When it came up for auction in the late
1960s, I thought how perfect it would
be if a nice Jewish girl like me were to
own it.

On being grateful for gifts

I mean, how many young women get a set of rubies just for doing something wholesome like swimming laps? Or win a diamond ring at Ping-Pong with their husband? Well, I did, and for all of these memories and the people in my life, I feel blessed.

I know I'm lucky. I know when I wear a lovely Dior gown and jewels and a nice hairstyle that I'm bloody lucky.

On owning jewelry

We are all temporary custodians of beauty.

Life without earrings is empty!

I adore wearing gems, but not because they are mine. You can't possess radiance, you can only admire it.

On diamonds

Big girls need big diamonds.

The price of food is going up…and diamonds, too.

You can't cry on a diamond's shoulder, and diamonds won't keep you warm at night, but they're sure fun when the sun shines!

Every breath
you take today
should be
with someone
else in mind.

VIII

GIVING BACK

In 1955, when MGM was deciding whether to allow Elizabeth to option out of her contract and star in *Giant* opposite Rock Hudson, Hudson fought for his choice for leading lady, and Elizabeth got the part. Her gratitude to Hudson was the thread of their lifelong friendship. The time they spent together both on and off the set was often filled with what Hudson described as many "liquid lunches." Their favorite drink? Chocolate martinis. Their favorite hangover cure? Bloody Marys. Admittedly, though, their hair-of-the-dog tactic often became the whole dog. When Hudson died from AIDS in 1985 at

age fifty-nine, Elizabeth was rocked to her core. Her wish was that he had not died in vain.

Though Elizabeth began fighting the stigma attached to AIDS in the early 1980s, it wasn't until Hudson's death that her work began in earnest. She recalled, "I kept seeing all these news reports on this new disease and kept asking myself why no one was doing anything. And then I realized that I was just like them. I wasn't doing anything to help." Shocked by her own inaction, she planned a fundraising dinner, the first major AIDS benefit, for AIDS Project Los Angeles (APLA). In 1985, Elizabeth joined with Dr. Mathilde Krim to form the American Foundation for AIDS Reseach (amfAR) and became the organization's first national chairman. Her participation in the fight against AIDS helped bring it to the forefront of media attention, and she discovered that Elizabeth Taylor, the commodity, could be put to good use.

In 1991, Elizabeth created the Elizabeth Taylor AIDS Foundation (ETAF), whose mission is to provide support for organizations that deliver direct care and services to AIDS patients, educate the public regarding AIDS, and conduct research to develop treatments and a cure. After a lifetime spent indulging her every whim, Elizabeth gave back in full. Like everything else in her life, she was passionate about her cause: Her generosity was overwhelming, and she reveled in her newfound role as philanthropist. Over the years, she raised millions of dollars for charity, fighting for the underchampioned, the sick, and the dispossessed.

Though she was awarded two Academy Awards for Best Actress, Elizabeth wanted most to be remembered for her charity work. In 2008, amfAR honored the veteran actress for her longstanding contribution to the fight against HIV/AIDS. Always one for a good fight, Elizabeth's goal to find a cure for AIDS may have been her most ambitious and rewarding challenge.

Page 210: Elizabeth,
circa 1958.

On the importance of giving

Giving is to give to God. Helping is to help others.

Nothing will raise your self-esteem as much as helping others. It will make you like yourself more and make you more likable. We can't all be Mother Teresa, but each of us can try to make our little corner of the earth better.

Celebrity is not something that comes without responsibility.

Remember always to give. That is the thing that will make you grow.

You are who you are. All you can do in this world is help others to be who they are and better themselves and those around them.

There's still so much more to do. I can't sit back and be complacent, and none of us should be. I get around now in a wheelchair, but I get around.

I have found that when you are not concerned with your own satisfaction or pleasure—only with giving—then you yourself receive so much more.

If not to make the world better, what is money for?

On fighting for gay rights

There is no such thing as a gay agenda. It's a human agenda.

Page 218: Elizabeth and Rock Hudson on the set of *Giant*, 1956.

On her work to find a cure for AIDS

Acting is, to me now, artificial. Seeing people suffer is real. It couldn't be more real. Some people don't like to look at it in the face because it's painful. But if nobody does, then nothing gets done.

I'm going to do everything in my power to make it happen.

I don't think President [George H. W.] Bush is doing enough about AIDS. In fact, I'm not even sure he knows how to spell AIDS.

It's bad enough that people are dying of AIDS, but no one should die of ignorance.

I could no longer take a passive role as I watched several people I knew and loved die a painful, slow, and lonely death.

I'm proudest of my charitable contri- butions. I've raised millions of dollars for the American Foundation for AIDS Research. And I'm not stopping here. I won't stop until that hideous disease is conquered.

I, along with
the critics,
have never
taken myself
very seriously.

IX

L LIFE

lizabeth's legendary performances, coupled with her intense beauty, passionate joie de vivre, stubborn spirit, and unapologetic lifestyle propelled her to an iconic status at an early age. Not only was she an original, but she was also a pioneer, albeit a controversial one, in both her personal and professional life.

The first woman to be paid one million dollars for a film—*Cleopatra*—Elizabeth set the stage for modern-day actresses, like Julia Roberts, to ask for more—and get it. Elizabeth's talent, perseverance, and strength of character inspired countless women, who considered her legendary life a model for their own, if only to borrow a page or two from her book. Elizabeth did what she wanted, when she wanted, and how she wanted, and most of the time, to everyone's amazement, including her own, she was able to pull it off. She did all of this without marginalizing her place in the Hollywood machine or pulling rank as diva; her professionalism remained intact, even when she struggled against illnesses and personal demons.

While her professional accomplishments were stunning, so too were the fairy-tale arcs of her torrid, sweeping love affairs. Yet for all the romances she conducted throughout the years, her most enduring one was with us, her public. Like a mad lover, we pushed her to the extremes of her limitations—all the while asking for more, more, more—and the free-willed, generous spirit that she was, she always gave back.

Page 222: Elizabeth, circa 1950.

On being naive

When you are young and you fall off
your cloud for the first time, you try
to make yourself believe everything is
still beautiful.

On perseverance

"Oh, I'm more determined than you
think. I'll win, all right."

—As Maggie, *Cat on a Hot Tin Roof*, 1958

On change

I think I've proven that anyone can change her life around and make it work. You only have to try.

On being passionate

Passion is the ingredient in me that has made me who I am. It's my passion for life…my passion for passion that has made me never give up.

Follow your passion, follow your heart, and the things you need will come.

The things that are important to me—being a mother, a businesswoman, an activist—are all things that were borne out of great passion.

I've
always
admitted
that
I'm
ruled
by
my
passions.

Elizabeth, circa 1952.

On morals

When the sun comes up,
I have morals again.

On humility

There's always this terrible danger,
when one talks about oneself, of sound-
ing like you're trying to capitalize on
your emotions, your relationships.

Always keep love and humility
in your heart.

On vices

The problem with people who have no vices is that generally you can be pretty sure they're going to have some pretty annoying virtues.

On the difference between real life and screen

In films, it seemed I could handle anything. I knew all the tricks. But this was confusing. The tricks could not be applied in real life.

ACKNOWLEDGMENTS

Immeasurable thanks to the two Elizabeths (Taylor and Sullivan) who made this book possible, and to Signe Bergstrom, Kate Blum, Ellen F. Brown, Kevin Callahan, Ryland Dodge, Brianne Halverson, Audra Honaker, Carrie Kania, Betsy Moss, Sam Pinkleton, Marta Schooler, Iris Shih, Katie Ukrop, and Amy Winegardner.

Elizabeth, 2002.

SELECT FILMOGRAPHY

* Denotes Academy Award for Best Actress

1951	*Callaway Went Thataway*
	Father's Little Dividend
	A Place in the Sun
	Quo Vadis?
1952	*Ivanhoe*
	Love Is Better Than Ever
1953	*The Girl Who Had Everything*
1954	*Beau Brummell*
	Elephant Walk
	The Last Time I Saw Paris
	Rhapsody
1956	*Giant*
1957	*Raintree County*
1958	*Cat on a Hot Tin Roof*
1959	*Suddenly, Last Summer*
1960	*BUtterfield 8* *
	Scent of Mystery
1963	*Cleopatra*
	The V.I.P.s
1965	*The Sandpiper*
1966	*Who's Afraid of Virginia Woolf?* *

BIBLIOGRAPHY

A & E Home Video. *Elizabeth Taylor Facets*. [United States]:
   A & E Home Video, 2002.

Amburn, E. *Elizabeth Taylor*. Oxford, England: Isis, 2001.

———. *The Most Beautiful Woman in the World: The Obsessions,
   Passions, and Courage of Elizabeth Taylor*. New York: Cliff
   Street Books, 2000.

BBC News. "Hollywood's Favourite Dame," December 31, 1999.

Bozzacchi, Gianni. *Elizabeth Taylor: The Queen and I*. Madison,
   Wisc.: University of Wisconsin Press, 2002.

Capote, Truman. *Portraits and Observations: The Essays of Truman
   Capote*. New York: Random House, 2007.

Christopher, James. *Elizabeth Taylor: The Biography*. Bath,
   England: Camden, 2002.

———. *Elizabeth Taylor: The Illustrated Biography*. London: Andre
   Deutsch, 1999.

Elizabeth Taylor AIDS Foundation. *Happy Birthday, Elizabeth: A
   Celebration of Life*. Hollywood, Calif.: Elizabeth Taylor AIDS
   Foundation, 1999.

Heymann, C. David. *Liz: An Intimate Biography of Elizabeth Taylor*.
   New York: Carol Publishing Group, 1995.

Hirsch, Foster. *Elizabeth Taylor*. New York: Galahad Books, 1975.

Howden, Iris. *Elizabeth Taylor*. London: Basic Skills Agency, 1994.

Hutchinson, Tom. *Elizabeth Taylor*. New York: Exeter Books, 1982.

Kelley, Kitty. *Elizabeth Taylor, The Last Star*. New York: Simon & Schuster, 1981.

Maddox, Brenda. *Who's Afraid of Elizabeth Taylor?* New York: M. Evans, 1977.

Mann, William J. *How to Be a Movie Star: Elizabeth Taylor in Hollywood*. Boston: Houghton Mifflin Harcourt, 2009.

Morley, Sheridan. *Elizabeth Taylor: A Celebration*. London: Pavilion, 1988.

Nickens, Christopher. *Elizabeth Taylor: A Biography in Photographs*. London: Hutchinson, 1984.

Pacific Rim, Ltd, BVS Productions, and Arts & Entertainment Network. *Elizabeth Taylor*, VHS. New York: 1993.

Sheppard, Dick. *Elizabeth: The Life and Career of Elizabeth Taylor*. Garden City, N.Y.: Doubleday, 1974.

Singer, Linda-Marie. *Elizabeth Taylor*. Philadelphia, Penn.: Chelsea House Publishers, 1999.

Spoto, Donald. *Elizabeth Taylor*. London: Little, Brown, 1995.

Taraborrelli, J. R. *Elizabeth*. New York: Warner Books, 2006.

Taylor, Elizabeth. *Elizabeth Taylor: An Informal Memoir*. New York: Harper & Row, 1965.

———. *Elizabeth Takes Off: On Weight Gain, Weight Loss, Self-image, and Self-esteem*. New York: Putnam, 1987.

———. *Elizabeth Taylor's Nibbles and Me*. New York: Simon & Schuster, 2002.

———, Richard Burton, et al. *Elizabeth Taylor Collection*, DVD. Woodland Hills, Calif.: St. Clair Vision, 2007.

———, Ruth A. Peltason, and John Bigelow Taylor. *Elizabeth Taylor: My Love Affair with Jewelry*. New York: Simon & Schuster, 2002.

———, interview by Arsenio Hall, *The Arsenio Hall Show*. CBS, June 11, 1992 (accessed via YouTube.com, February 24, 2011).

———, interview by Barbara Walters, *Barbara Walters Special*, ABC, March 30, 1987 (accessed via YouTube.com, April 1, 2010).

———, interview by Gary Collins, *Hour Magazine*, Group W. Productions, August 21–25, 1987 (accessed via YouTube.com, February 24, 2011).

———, interview by Larry King, *Larry King Live*, CNN, January 15, 2001. CNN Transcripts: www.cnn.com (accessed via YouTube.com, December 12, 2010).

Thiltges, Alexander. *Elizabeth Taylor: A Life in Pictures*. London: Pavilion, 2008.

Thompson, Thomas. *Life* magazine, January 17, 1969.

Ursini, James. *Taylor*. Köln: Taschen, 2008.

Vermilye, Jerry and Mark Ricci. *The Films of Elizabeth Taylor*. Secaucus, N.J.: Citadel Press, 1976.

Walker, Alexander. *Elizabeth: The Life of Elizabeth Taylor*. New York: Grove Weidenfeld, 1991.

Waterbury, Ruth. *Elizabeth Taylor*. New York: Appleton-Century, 1964.

Willoughby, Bob. *Liz: An Intimate Collection: Photographs of Elizabeth Taylor*. London: Merrell, 2004.

PHOTOGRAPHY
CREDITS